Twenty to Make
Mini Bunting

Alistair Macdonald

Search Press

First published in Great Britain 2014

Search Press Limited
Wellwood, North Farm Road,
Tunbridge Wells, Kent TN2 3DR

Text copyright © Alistair MacDonald 2013

Photographs by Paul Bricknell
at Search Press Studios

Photographs and design copyright
© Search Press Ltd 2013

Print ISBN: 978-1-78221-004- 7
Epub ISBN: 978-1-78126-199-6
Mobi ISBN: 978-1-78126-200-9
PDF ISBN: 978-1-78126-201-6

Suppliers
If you have difficulty in obtaining any of the
materials and equipment mentioned in this
book, then please visit the Search Press website
for details of suppliers: www.searchpress.com

Printed in China

*I would like to dedicate this book to my
Mum and Iain.*

Contents

Introduction

From an early age I remember bunting; whether draping the stalls at a country fair, or flapping in the wind while on a summer holiday at the seaside, or hanging on the walls to mark the end of the year at the school disco. Bunting is not just a humble decoration – it can be used to redecorate a whole room or transform a garden space so that a special occasion is remembered for ever.

Bunting can be made from virtually anything and it is a fantastic way of using up the fabric scraps and hoarded bits and pieces that we just can't seem to part with! Our belief that everything will have a use 'one day' can become a reality with bunting. With a bit of imagination, the plainest fabric can be transformed into something quite magical. Crafting your own tailor-made bunting for a specific occasion can give you immense satisfaction. It could be a seasonal holiday or a family celebration; and sometimes you don't even have to have a reason. Mini bunting is so tiny and versatile that it can cheer up any space all year round!

In this book you will find something for everyone – adult or child, boy or girl. Make them 'walk the plank' with the Pirate bunting, relax in the summer with Busy Bees bunting or simply count down the days to Christmas with super cute Advent Stockings. There is something for everyone and they're a joy to make.

All of the designs are easy to follow and come with step-by-step instructions as well as templates to help you along. You don't have to be a professional – just have a go. Sewing should be fun after all!

So what's stopping you? Clear the kitchen table and get creative.

Happy sewing!

Techniques

For the projects that follow, all you need are some simple hand and machine sewing techniques. To help you with some of the more decorative stitching methods and preparing your work before 'turning through', take a look at the following notes and diagrams.

Blanket stitch

 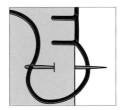 

1 With the thread secured on the reverse of the fabric, bring the needle to the front and pierce through your stitching line. The needle should be pointing away from the edge of the work. Loop the working thread underneath the needle.

2 Pull the needle entirely through the work and tighten the stitch. Repeat Step 1, keeping the thread tension consistent.

3 Keep stitching along the required parts of the work, equally spacing the stitches to produce a neat finish. Do not pull the thread too tightly, as it will distort the work.

Chain stitch

  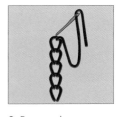

1 At the start of the sewing line, secure the thread on the reverse side and bring the needle through the fabric. Always hold the thread towards the left-hand side in the direction you are sewing. Insert the needle directly beside the thread you have just pulled through. Bring the needle back through to the front and above the initial entry point. Loop the thread under the needle tip from right to left and continue to pull the needle all the way through.

2 Adjust the loop shape and tension if required. Insert the needle again just to the left of the previous exit point and bring it back through towards the top. Loop the thread under the needle and pull through to form another loop.

3 Repeat the process until your chain is the desired length. To finish, simply stitch over the top of the last loop and tie the thread off at the back.

Slip stitch

1 Start by securing the thread to the back of one of the pieces of fabric and bring through to the front. With the thread through one of the pieces to be joined, place the needle through the other. During this motion, only pick up a few threads.

2 Pull the needle all the way through, bringing the thread with it. Repeat this process but alternate the stitches along both sides of the join.

3 Pull the thread gently as you stitch to maintain tension. Do not pull too tightly as this will cause the work to pucker.

Clipping

This is a necessary step to allow the fabric you are using to form the desired shape when you turn it through (clipping releases the space the fabric needs to form the shape intended).

Clipping points: Start by cutting a straight line just below the point of the stitch line. If you cut too far away, the point will not be sharp enough – cut too close and the danger is that when easing the point out, it will fray and open up. Trim back the seam allowance either side of the point.

Clipping corners: Trim off the point of each corner just above the point that has been stitched. Some thicker fabrics may also require you to shave off some of the seam allowance either side of this point.

Clipping curves: The best way to clip a curve is to cut small triangular notches into the seam allowance around the curve you want to form. The tip of each notch should be cut close to the stitching – be careful not to cut through the stitching line. On the sharper curves, you will need more notches (fewer notches if the curve is smoother).

Clipping heart shapes: See above for curves. For the central point, you will need one single, inverted notch in order to achieve a true heart shape when turned through.

Using the templates

Other than the two main bunting templates below, where required, you will find any specific templates on each project page. To make a full-size template, enlarge the template on a printer or photocopier to the specified size. Use each template for both layers of fabric.

Triangle template.
Enlarge to 200%.

Rectangle template.
Enlarge to 200%.

Floral Bunting

Materials:

Card for template

For each flag you will need a 12 x 10cm (4¾ x 4in) piece of floral fabric (I have used Liberty print)

The same for the lining in either calico or corresponding colour cotton

Floral bias binding 2.5cm (1in) wide, measure to the desired length of the bunting, plus ties at the ends

Sewing thread to match the bias binding

Tools:

Pencil

Ruler

Fabric marker

Pins

Scissors, both paper and fabric

Iron

Sewing machine

Large upholstery needle or knitting needle

Instructions:

1 Transfer the triangle template (page 7) on to some card and cut it out.

2 Lay the desired floral fabric, right side down, on to the lining fabric and secure it with pins. Place the template on to the cloth and mark all of the edges with a fabric marker. Secure the two layers of the flag with pins and cut round the marked lines. Repeat this process until you have enough flags for your bunting length.

3 Set a sewing machine to a medium-sized stitch. Take a flag and start to sew down one of the sides. Seam allowance has been added to the template at 1cm (³/₈in). As you reach the end of the first side, stop the stitching 1cm (³/₈in) away from the base of the work. Lift the foot and turn the flag towards you. This will align the opposite side to continue stitching. Now clip the excess fabric from the tip of the flag (see page 7) and turn right side out. Use the eye of a large upholstery or knitting needle to ease the tip of the flag out (take care not to push too hard as this may result in the needle coming through the work). Press the flag flat and trim away the protruding seam allowance to maintain a straight edge along the top of the flag. Repeat this process until all the flags have been completed.

4 Using an iron, take the bias binding and carefully press in half lengthwise, matching the edges together. Sandwich each flag between the folded bias and pin into position, spacing evenly as you go; my flags are 7.5cm (3in) apart. Make sure you leave enough free bias at the start and finish to allow for ties. Sew along the entire bunting close to the edge of the bias binding using a sewing machine set to a medium straight stitch. Stitch as close to the edge as you can.

5 Press the finished bunting and hang it up.

Mistletoe Bunting

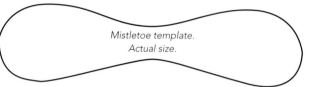

Materials:

Card for template

Dark and light green felt for leaves

Large pearl sewing beads for the fruits, approx. 10mm (³/₈in) diameter

Red cotton bias binding 2cm (¾in) wide, measure to the required length of the bunting, plus ties at the ends

Sewing thread to match the bias binding

Tools:

Pencil

Fabric marker

Scissors, both paper and fabric

Iron

Sewing machine

Hand sewing needle

Mistletoe template.
Actual size.

Instructions:

1 Start by folding the bias binding in half lengthwise, and press closed with an iron, taking care to match the edges together. Using the sewing thread, machine sew a medium straight stitch along the entire strip of bias binding as close to the edge as you can. Finish the ends by machine sewing a satin or zigzag stitch and trim.

2 Now mark the position of each sprig of mistletoe with a fabric marker. I have spaced mine 13cm (5in) apart. Count all the marks. This will give you the exact number of sprigs to be cut out.

3 Transfer the mistletoe template on to card and use it to cut out one light green and one dark green felt leaf. Cut the same for each mistletoe sprig required.

4 Fold the spigs of mistletoe at an angle to create the effect of a cluster. By hand, sew the leaves into position along the bias strip. Hand stitch three large pearl beads to the centre of each cluster.

Christmas Bunting

Materials:

Card for template

Red and green floral fabric (I have used Liberty); 10 x 12cm (4 x 4¾in) per flag and the same to use as a lining

Large red jacket buttons

Red bias binding 2cm (¾in) wide, measure to the desired length of the bunting, plus ties at the ends

Green embroidery thread

Sewing thread to match the bias binding

Tools:

Pencil

Ruler

Fabric marker

Pins

Scissors, both paper and fabric

Iron

Sewing machine

Large upholstery needle or knitting needle

Hand sewing needle

Instructions:

1 Start by transferring the triangle template (page 7) on to card and cut it out.

2 With the fabric pinned right sides together, place the template on top and carefully draw around all of the edges using a fabric marker. Remove the template and secure the two layers together with pins, then cut round the marked lines. Repeat this process until you have enough flags for your bunting length.

3 Set a sewing machine to a medium-sized stitch. Take a flag and start to sew down one of the sides. Seam allowance has been added to the template at 1cm (³/₈in). As you reach the end of the first side, stop the stitching 1cm (³/₈in) away from the base of the work. Lift the foot and turn the flag towards you and continue stitching down the opposite edge. Now clip the excess fabric from the tip of the flag (see page 7) and turn right side out. Use the eye of a large upholstery or knitting needle to ease the tip of the flag out. Take care not to push too hard as this may result in the needle coming through the work. Press the flag flat and trim away the protruding seam allowance to maintain a straight edge along the top. Repeat this process until all of the flags have been completed.

4 Using an iron, carefully press the bias binding in half lengthwise, matching the edges together. Sandwich each flag between the folded bias and pin into position. Space evenly and alternate red flags with green flags; I have spaced mine 2.5cm (1in) apart. Make sure you leave enough free bias at the start and finish to allow for ties. Sew the bias binding together along the entire length using a sewing machine set to a medium straight stitch. Stitch as close to the edge as you can. Press the bunting flat.

5 Between each flag, hand sew a red jacket button in the centre of the bias binding using green embroidery thread.

Pirate Bunting

Materials:

Card for templates

Black and white felt

Red and white striped cotton, two 10 x 12cm (4 x 4¾in) pieces per triangle flag, and two 8 x 11cm (3¼ x 4¼in) pieces per rectangle flag

Navy and white striped cotton, flags as above

Black cotton with white stars, for triangle flags as above

Gold braid, approx. 30cm (11¾in) per rope detail

Large and medium white buttons

Blue and black sewing thread

Black bias binding 2cm (¾in) wide, measure to the required length of the bunting, plus ties at the ends

Tools:

Pencil

Ruler

Fabric marker

Pins

Scissors, both paper and fabric

Iron

Sewing machine

Large upholstery needle or knitting needle

Hand sewing needle

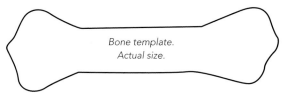

Bone template.
Actual size.

Instructions:

1 Start by transferring the triangle and rectangle templates (page 7) on to card and cut them out.

2 Each flag is equally spaced at 2.5cm (1in) apart. Work out your desired length of the finished bunting and how many of each flag you will require. The repeat pattern for this bunting is as follows, red-striped triangle, navy-striped rectangle, skull-and-cross-bones flag, black and white star triangle and finishing with a red and white striped rectangle.

3 With the fabrics pinned right sides together, draw around the templates using a fabric marker. Remove the templates and secure the layers with pins. Cut around the marked lines. Repeat this process for all the flags required.

4 Set a sewing machine to a medium-sized stitch. Take a triangle flag and start to sew down one of the sides. Seam allowance has been added to the template at 1cm (³/₈in). As you reach the end of the first side, stop the stitching 1cm (³/₈in) away from the base of the work. Lift the foot and turn the flag towards you and continue stitching down the opposite edge. Now clip the excess fabric from the tip of the flag (see page 7) and turn right side out. Use the end of a large upholstery needle or knitting needle to ease the tip of the flag out. Press the flag flat and trim away the protruding seam allowance to maintain a straight edge along the top of the flag. Repeat this process for the rectangle templates until you have the right number of cotton shapes.

5 To make the skull-and-cross-bones flags, cut rectangles in felt measuring 6 x 11cm (2¼ x 4¼in). Use the bone template and cut two bones per rectangle. Hand stitch the bones crossed on to the black rectangle then hand stitch one medium-sized button towards the base of the cross. Overlap the larger button to finish and form the skull (refer to image).

6 Once all of the flags are ready, using an iron, carefully press the bias binding in half lengthwise, matching the edges together. Sandwich each flag between the folded bias and pin into position, spacing evenly 2.5cm (1in) apart. Make sure you leave enough free bias at the start and finish to allow for ties. Press the bunting flat. With blue thread, sew the bias binding together along the entire length using a sewing machine set to a medium straight stitch. Stitch as close to the edge as you can. Cut the gold braid into 30cm (11¾in) strips and tie each end in a knot. Loop together to form coils and attach to the bias binding using black thread.

Gingham Bunting

Materials:

Card for template

Assorted colours of cotton gingham fabric, 10 x 12cm (4 x 4¾in) required per flag, and the same to use as a lining

Crochet balls 2.5cm (1in) diameter

Pale sewing thread to tone with fabric

Tools:

Pencil

Ruler

Fabric marker

Pins

Scissors, both paper and fabric

Sewing machine

Large upholstery needle or knitting needle

Hand sewing needle

Instructions:

1 Use the triangle template (page 7) to transfer the shape on to card and cut it out.

2 Decide on a finished length for this quirky bunting, with the desired amount of flags. Follow steps 2 and 3 of Christmas bunting (page 12). However when it comes to stitching on the sewing machine you need to start stitching along the top of the straight edge leaving a gap in the middle of each flag to allow turning through (see the stitching guide in the template on page 7). This project does not use bias binding so you will need to finish the tops of the flags.

3 Once the flags are turned through and pressed, use a slip stitch (see the stitching guide in the template on page 7) and pale sewing thread to close the opening.

4 Join the flags together by sewing each end to a crochet ball. Continue until you have reached your desired length.

Nautical Bunting

Materials:

Card for templates

Cotton fabric in blue tonal shades and
navy/white striped cotton for triangle flags,
10 x 12cm (4 x 4¾in) – cut two per flag

Cotton fabric in blue tonal shades for
rectangle flags, 8 x 11cm (3¼ x 4¼in)
– cut two per flag

Blue sewing thread

Blue bias binding 2cm (¾in) wide, measure to
the required length of the bunting, plus ties
at the ends

Tools:

Pencil

Ruler

Fabric marker

Pins

Scissors, both paper and fabric

Iron

Sewing machine

Large upholstery needle or knitting needle

Hand sewing needle

Instructions:

1 Transfer the rectangle and triangle templates (see page 7) on to card and cut them
out. Each repeat of the flags (as shown in the photograph) will make approximately
53cm (20¾in) of bunting.

2 Lay the fabrics together with the right sides facing each other. Pin to secure them.
Draw round the templates using a fabric marker. Remove the templates and secure
the layers with pins. Cut around the marked lines. Repeat this process for all the
flags required.

3 Set a sewing machine to a medium-sized stitch. Take a triangle flag and start to
sew down one of the sides with a seam allowance of 1cm (³⁄₈in). As you reach the end
of the first side, stop the stitching 1cm (½in) away from the base of the work. Lift the
foot and turn the flag towards you. This will align the next side to continue stitching.
Now clip the excess fabric from the tips of the flag (see page 7) and turn right side out.
Use the end of a large upholstery needle or knitting needle to ease the tips of the flag
out, but don't push too hard. Press the flag flat and trim away the protruding seam
allowance to maintain a straight edge along the top of the flag. Repeat this process
for all the triangles and rectangles.

4 Using an iron, press the bias binding in half lengthwise, taking care to match the edges for a neat finish. Leave enough bias binding at both ends to form the ties and begin to place the flags into position. Sandwich each flag between the bias binding and secure with pins following the pattern shown. Each flag should be 2.5cm (1in) apart from the overlapping triangles. Hand sew these together before placing into the binding.

5 Once you are happy with the arrangement and spacing, sew the bias binding together, closing and trapping the flags inside. Use blue thread to machine sew a medium straight stitch. Stitch as close to the edge as you can.

Tweed Bunting

Materials:

Card for template

An assortment of tweed wool fabrics, triangle flags require 10 x 12cm (4 x 4¾in) – cut two per flag

Yellow sewing thread

Yellow bias binding 2cm (¾in) wide, measure to the required length of the bunting, plus ties at the ends

Tools:

Pencil

Ruler

Fabric marker

Pins

Scissors, both paper and fabric

Iron

Sewing machine

Large upholstery needle or knitting needle

Instructions:

1 Transfer the triangle template on to card and cut it out (see page 7).

2 With the right sides of the tweed facing each other, lay flat and secure with pins. Place the template on to the fabric and mark all the edges with a fabric marker. Remove the template, secure the two layers with pins and cut round the marked lines. Repeat this process until you have enough flags for your bunting length.

3 Take each flag and start to sew down one of the sides using a medium-sized stitch on your sewing machine. As you reach the end of the first side, stop the stitching 1cm (³/₈in) away from the base of the work. Lift the foot and turn the flag towards you. This will align

the opposite side to continue stitching. Now clip the excess fabric from the tip of the flag (see page 7) and turn right side out. Use the eye of a large upholstery needle or knitting needle to ease the tip of the flag out. Take care not to push too hard as this may result in the needle coming through the work. Press the flag flat and trim away the protruding seam allowance to maintain a straight edge along the top of the flag. Repeat this process until all of the flags have been completed.

4 Press the bias binding in half lengthwise with an iron, matching the edges together. Sandwich each flag between the folded bias and pin into position, spacing evenly as you go; I have spaced mine 4cm (1½in) apart. Make sure you leave enough free bias at the start and finish to allow for ties. Using a sewing machine set to a medium straight stitch, sew along the entire binding edge, closing and trapping the flags inside. Stitch as close to the edge as you can.

5 Press the finished bunting and hang it up.

Busy Bees Bunting

Materials:

Card for template

Baby pink felt for large petal 10 x 12cm
(4 x 4¾in) per petal

Fuschia pink felt for small petal 6 x 8cm
(2¼ x 3¼in) per petal

For the bumble bee: two small black
pom-poms, one medium yellow
pom-pom, and a small scrap of white
felt for the wings

Pink and white sewing thread

Black and purple embroidery thread

Black buttons (size 24 line)

Baby pink bias binding 2cm (¾in) wide,
measure to the required length of the
bunting, plus ties at the ends

Tools:

Pencil

Fabric marker

Pins

Scissors, both paper and
fabric

Iron

Sewing machine

Hand sewing
needle

*Bee's wing
template.
Actual size.*

*Petal templates.
Enlarge to 200%.*

Instructions:

1 Start by determining the length of bunting. Two flowers, with a spacing of 7cm (2¾in) between them, should produce approximately 26cm (10¼in) of bunting. This should help you decide how many flowers you will need to make.

2 Transfer the petal templates on to card and cut them out. Pin them on to the correct colour of felt and carefully cut round each one. Cut as many as you will need.

3 Thread a needle with purple embroidery thread and apply some decorative long stitches on the smaller petals, starting from the centre and working out in a random fashion. Once you feel there is enough definition to emulate the centre of a flower, sew the larger petal to the back of the smaller petal in the centre, using the purple thread. Sew a black button through the centre of both layers, securing it at the back. Repeat until all flowers are complete.

4 Using an iron, press the entire length of the bias binding in half, taking care to match the edges for a neat finish. Set a sewing machine to a medium-sized stitch and sew the bias closed as close to the edge as you can. Press flat.

5 Pin all the flowers in position and hand sew to secure them using white thread. Add some extra character to some of the flowers by bringing the edge of the larger petals slightly closer to the centre of the flower and sew them to the bias binding with a few stitches. This creates a 3D waved effect.

6 Making the bumble bees is easy! Thread a needle with the black embroidery thread and tie a knot at the end. Sew through a black pom-pom and then the yellow and finish with another black. Come back though the last black pom-pom. Make as many bumble bees as you like in this way. Next, transfer the bee's wing template on to card and cut it out. Pin it to some felt and carefully cut as many wings as required. Using black thread, hand sew the little set of wings on the yellow pom-pom. The finished bumble bees can then be hand sewn with black thread to your flowers.

Irish Bunting

Materials:

Card for templates

Green and dark green cotton fabric

Green and white striped cotton for triangle
flags, 10 x 12cm (4 x 4¾) – cut two per flag;
and for rectangle flags, 8 x 11cm (3¼ x 4¼in)
– cut two per flag

Green sewing thread

Copper-coloured shirt buttons

Green embroidery thread

Green and light green felt scraps

Green bias binding 2cm (¾in) wide, measure to
the required length of the bunting, plus ties
at the ends

Tools:

Pencil

Ruler

Fabric marker

Pins

Scissors, both paper and fabric

Iron

Sewing machine

Large upholstery needle or knitting needle

Hand sewing needle

*Shamrock template.
Actual size.*

Instructions:

1 Transfer the rectangle and triangle templates on to card (see page 7). Cut the templates out. Each repeat of flags will make approximately 56cm (22in) of bunting.

2 Follow steps 2–4 of the Nautical bunting on pages 18–19, but without the overlapping triangles.

3 Once you are happy with the arrangement, use an iron to fold and press the the bias binding in half lengthwise, taking care to match the edges. Machine sew the bias closed using green thread and medium-sized stitches, securing the flags inside. Try and sew as close to the edge as you can.

4 Now comes the fun part! To decorate the flags with shamrocks, start by threading a needle with green embroidery thread and use a chain stitch (see page 6) to create the stalks. In the meantime, use the shamrock template to cut out enough felt shapes as required. Sew these in alternating colours to the green rectangle flags at the top of your stalks. Add three of the buttons to each felt shamrock and four to the striped cotton flags without felt.

Valentine Bunting

Materials:

Card for template

Red and cream cotton; each heart will need a 12 x 12cm (4¾ x 4¾in) square and the same again as a lining

Polyester wadding, 2cm (¾in) thick

Red grosgrain ribbon, 9cm (3½in) long per heart

Red and white sewing threads

Red bias binding 2cm (¾in) wide, measure to the required length of the bunting, plus ties at the ends

Tools:

Pencil

Ruler

Chalk fabric marker

Pins

Scissors, both paper and fabric

Iron

Sewing machine

Large upholstery needle or knitting needle

Hand sewing needle

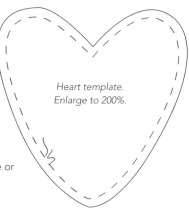

Heart template. Enlarge to 200%.

Instructions:

1 Transfer the heart template on to some card then cut it out.

2 Cut both cottons (red and white) into 12 x 12cm (4¾ x 4¾in) squares. Put half of these to one side for linings. Place each remaining square, right side up on to the wadding and sew a large running stitch all the way round. This will stop the two pieces sliding when quilting. Use a chalk marker to draw a grid of 2 x 2cm (¾ x ¾in) squares on the diagonal so they will appear diamond shaped on the finished hearts.

3 Set a sewing machine to a medium stitch length and topstitch over the marker lines. Use a contrasting thread for impact. Finish all squares in the same manner.

4 Place the lining squares and the quilted squares right sides together and pin together matching up all four corners. Using the template and a chalk marker, draw around the heart in the centre of each square and place three extra pins inside the heart. Do not cut anything off at this stage.

5 Using the side of the foot on the sewing machine as a guide, sew round the whole of the inside of the heart. Cut around the stitch lines leaving 5mm (¼in) seam allowance. Lightly clip into the top of the heart to avoid twisting when turning through (see page 7).

6 With the unquilted side facing you, slash a straight vertical line about 5cm (2in) long with the fabric scissors. You now have an opening in which to turn the work through. Use a large upholstery needle or knitting needle to ease the shape of the heart to its full potential. Do not press the hearts with an iron as this will flatten them. To cover up the slashed opening, draw the fabric together with a large rough stitch. Cover the drawn hole using the grosgrain ribbon. Slip stitch the grosgrain ribbon in place for neatness (see page 7).

7 Press the red bias binding in half lengthwise, matching edge to edge. Set a sewing machine to a medium straight stitch and sew the bias closed as close to the edge as you can. Press flat. Pin the hearts to the bias at the desired spacing and slip stitch (see page 7) to the bias tape.

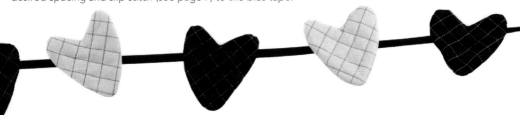

Japanese Silk Bunting

Materials:

Card for template

Chinese/Japanese silk, 9cm x 12cm (3½ x 4¾in) for each purse and the same again as a lining

Turquoise embroidery thread

Small turquoise tassels, one for each purse

Thread to match the silk

Gold braid the length of the finished bunting plus 10cm (4in) extra per loop

Cloth for ironing

Tools:

Pencil

Ruler

Fabric marker

Pins

Scissors, both paper and fabric

Iron

Sewing machine

Large upholstery needle or knitting needle

Hand sewing needle

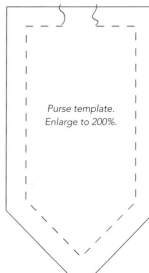

Purse template. Enlarge to 200%.

Instructions:

1 Transfer the template on to card and cut it out. Lay your chosen silks one on top of each other, right sides facing. Draw around the amount of purses required and cut two layers. It is a good idea to pin down the pieces before you cut as the silk will slip and slide.

2 With the cut-outs pinned together, set a sewing machine to a medium-sized straight stitch and start to sew along the top of the purse. Follow the indicated stitch lines, leaving a gap to enable the work to be turned through. Carefully clip the tips and turn right side out. Gently tease the corners out with a large upholstery needle or knitting needle. Press flat with a cloth covering the silk to protect it. Repeat to make all the purses.

3 Thread a needle with thread to match the silk. Close the opening using a slip stitch (see page 7). Hand sew a tassel on to the end of each purse tip and set aside.

4 Prepare the gold braid on which the purses are to hang. Make a knot in one end of the braid and leave enough slack for a tie before you start the first loop. Mark out 10cm (4in) of braid with two pins and bring the pins together to form a loop. Use turquoise embroidery thread to secure the loop by wrapping it through the loop and over the top. Secure the thread. Mark a gap of 10cm (4in) where the purse will hang. Repeat the loop process. Stop this process once you have enough spaces to hang all the purses. Remember to finish with a loop after the last purse for symmetry.

5 Fold each purse over the braid and pin into position. Secure by hand sewing the front to the back of the purse just below the braid using thread to match the silk.

Advent Stockings Bunting

Materials:

Card for templates

Red cotton velvet, two pieces
13cm x 15cm (5 x 6in)
for each stocking.

Red cotton, two pieces as
above for the lining

Toy stuffing

White felt for the numbers

3mm (1/8in) red and green
ribbon for ties

4cm (1½in) wide white satin
ribbon; 9cm (3½in)
per stocking

Red and white sewing thread

Green bias binding 2cm
(¾in) wide, measure to
the required length of the
bunting, plus ties at the
ends

Fabric glue

Tools:

Pencil

Fabric marker

Pins

Scissors, both paper and fabric

Computer and printer

Iron

Sewing machine

Tweezers

Hand sewing needle

Instructions:

1 On a computer enlarge numbers 1–25 in a bold font (perhaps a font size of about 85). Print this off and use as templates to cut out the numbers for the stockings in white felt. Pin through each number to hold in place as you cut. Put to one side.

2 Make a copy of the stocking template. Mark out twenty-five stockings in red velvet and cut two layers for each. Repeat this process using red cotton for the linings. Lay all of the stocking pieces flat on a bench with the velvet side facing you. Separate the stockings into two piles – all of the ones pointing to your left on one side and the ones to the right in another. Start with the ones pointing to the left. For each stocking top, cut off a length of white satin ribbon and stitch in place along the top. With the ribbon in place, top stitch the remaining loose edge which runs horizontally across the stocking. Trim the excess of the ribbon away. Now take the corresponding red cotton lining and, with right sides facing, pin the two layers along the top and machine stitch this edge together. Fold out as though you are opening a book and lightly press the seam allowance away from the velvet towards the cotton. Repeat this process twenty-five times.

3 As above, but without the white ribbon, repeat the process another twenty-five times with the remaining pile of stockings that are pointing to the right.

*Stocking template.
Enlarge to 200%.*

4 Pair all of the stockings together with the right sides facing each other. Make sure you match cotton to cotton and velvet to velvet. Use the stitched lines as placement guides. Pin securely to avoid slipping. Machine stitch around the entire work leaving the toe of the cotton side open to enable turning through and stuffing. Clip into the curves of the seam allowance. Finish all twenty-five in the same way.

5 Turn the stockings right side out and invert the cotton to line the sock. Fill the toe with a little stuffing. Repeat process.

6 Finish the length of the green bias binding by using an iron to press in half lengthwise and machine stitch closing the bottom edge. Use a red thread to contrast with the green and stitch, as close to the edge as you can. With fabric glue and tweezers, glue the felt numbers on to the stockings and allow to dry fully. Thread a needle with 3mm (1/8in) ribbon, sew through the top of each stocking (alternate red and green) and secure on to the prepared bias binding ties with a pretty bow. Fill each stocking with toy stuffing and sweets and count down the days!

Bow Tie Bunting

Materials:

Card for templates

An assortment of cotton fabric in bright colours 8 x 11cm (3¼ x 4¼in) for rectangle flags – cut two per flag

Fancy striped ribbon for bows 4cm (1½in) wide and 23cm (9in) for each bow

Yellow sewing thread

2cm (½in) wide bias binding scraps for the middle of bow ties

Yellow bias binding 2cm (¾in) wide, measure to the required length of the bunting, plus ties at the ends

Tools:

Pencil

Ruler

Fabric marker

Pins

Scissors, both paper and fabric

Iron

Sewing machine

Large upholstery needle or knitting needle

Hand sewing needle

Instructions:

1 Transfer the rectangle template (page 7) on to card and cut it out.

2 With right sides facing, place the fabrics on top of each other. Pin the template on to the fabric and draw round all of the edges with a fabric marker. Remove the template and secure the layers with pins. Cut around the marked lines. Repeat this process for all flags required.

3 Set a sewing machine to a medium-sized stitch. Take a flag and start to sew down one of the sides with a seam allowance of 1cm (³/₈in). As you reach the end of the first side, stop the stitching 1cm (³/₈in) away from the base of the work. Lift the foot and turn the flag towards you (anti-clockwise). This will align the next side to continue stitching. Once completely sewn, clip the excess fabric from the tips of the rectangle (see page 7) and turn right side out. Use the end of a large upholstery needle or knitting needle to ease the tips of the flag out. Press flat. Repeat this process until all of the flags have been completed.

4 With a hot iron, press the entire length of the bias binding in half lengthwise, taking care to match the edges for a neat finish. Leave enough bias binding at both ends to form the ties. You can now begin to place the flags into position. Sandwich each flag between the binding and secure with pins. Each flag should be 8cm (3¼in) apart.

5 Once you are happy with the arrangement, machine sew the bias binding together using yellow thread, closing the flags in place. Sew as close to the edge as you can.

6 To make the bow ties, cut your chosen fancy ribbon into 23cm (9in) strips. Place a pin in the middle of each strip to act as a guide. Bring the ends of the ribbon towards the centre, edge to edge, and sew down to secure along both raw edges (machine stitching is fine). Now bring the top and bottom long edges into the centre and secure at the central point. Flip the work right side up and lightly fold in half once again lengthways (this will concertina the centre of the ribbon, narrowing it to form our bow tie shape). Wrap a scrap of bias binding or ribbon around the middle and slip stitch closed, forming the 'knot' of the bow tie. Make sure you close the tape on the underside of the bow tie, which will be hidden.

7 Place the completed bow ties in the middle of each flag and pin. Secure in position by tacking down the four outer corners of the 'knot'. Plump up the outer parts (wings) of the bow ties.

Vintage Style Bunting

Materials:

Card for template

For each flag you will need 12 x 10cm (4¾ x 4in) of floral fabric (I have used a Liberty print), plain cotton for the lining and some white/ivory lace

Pink bias binding 2.5cm (1in) wide, measure to the required length of the bunting, plus ties at the ends

Light pink or white sewing thread

Tools:

Pencil

Ruler

Fabric marker

Pins

Scissors, both paper and fabric

Iron

Sewing machine

Large upholstery needle or knitting needle

Instructions:

1 Transfer the triangle template (page 7) on to some card and cut it out.

2 Lay the three fabrics on top of each other: floral fabric facing up, lace facing up and lastly the plain cotton face down as the top layer. Pin the template on to the fabric layers and mark all the edges with a fabric marker. Remove the template and secure the three layers with pins. Cut around the marked lines. Repeat this process until you have enough flags for your chosen bunting length.

3 Set a sewing machine to a medium-sized stitch. Take a flag and start to sew down one of the sides trapping all three layers together, seam allowance added at 1cm (½in). As you reach the end of the first side, stop the stitching 1cm away from the base of the work. Lift the foot and turn the flag towards you (anti-clockwise). This will align the opposite side to continue stitching. Now trim/clip the excess fabric from the flag (see page 7) and fold through turning right side out. The lace fabric should be facing you with the floral fabric underneath. Use a large upholstery needle or knitting needle to ease the tip of the flag out. Take care not to push too hard as this may result in the needle coming through the work. Press the flag flat and trim away the protruding seam allowance to maintain a straight edge along the top of the flag. Repeat this process until all of the flags have been completed.

4 Take the bias binding and carefully press it in half lengthwise, matching the edges together. Sandwich each flag between the folded bias and pin into position, spacing evenly as you go; I have spaced mine 2.5cm (1in) apart. Make sure you leave enough free bias at the start and finish to allow for ties. Machine sew, using light pink or white thread, along the entire bunting length with a medium straight stitch. Stitch as close to the edge as you can.

5 Press the finished bunting and hang it up.

Yoyo Flower Bunting

Materials:

For each large yoyo you will need
20 x 20cm (7¾ x 7¾in) plain cotton and floral fabric (I have used a 'Liberty' floral print).

For each smaller yoyo you will need 12 x 12cm (4¾ x 4¾in) of each fabric

Cream bias binding 2.5cm (1in) wide, measure to the required length of the bunting, plus ties at the ends

Cream or matching pale sewing thread

Tools:

Pins

Scissors, both paper and fabric

Iron

Sewing machine

Large and medium yoyo makers, available from craft or sewing suppliers

Yoyo maker, available from craft and sewing suppliers

Hand sewing needle

Instructions:

1 Each yoyo flower requires one large and one small finished yoyo. Two flowers spaced 8cm (3¼in) apart, makes 24cm (9½in) of bunting. Work out the total number of yoyos required for your finished bunting and cut out using the yoyo maker as a template.

2 Assemble all of the yoyos following the manufacturer's instructions. Place a small yoyo into the centre of a large one and hand sew straight through the middle, securing at the rear of the larger yoyo.

3 Prepare the length of cream bias binding by pressing in half lengthwise, and machine stitching down using a matching thread. Stitch as close to the edge as you can.

4 Pin each finished flower on to the binding, spaced 8cm (3¼in) apart. On the reverse of the binding, slip stitch the flowers into position (see page 7).

Kite Bunting

Materials:

Card for template

An assortment of bright gingham and solid coloured cotton fabric, 10 x 16cm (4 x 6¼in) for each kite

Cream cotton fabric, 10 x 16cm (4 x 6¼in) for each lining

Polyester wadding 2cm (¾in) thick

Assorted colours of grosgrain ribbon, approximately 50cm (19¾in) per kite

Blue sewing thread

Sky blue bias binding 2cm (¾in) wide, measure to the required length of the bunting, plus ties at the ends

Tools:

Pencil

Ruler

Fabric marker

Pins

Scissors, both paper and fabric

Iron

Sewing machine

Large upholstery needle or knitting needle

Hand sewing needle

Instructions:

1 Transfer the kite template on to card and cut it out.

2 Cut the bright plain cottons into 10 x 16cm (4 x 6¼in) rectangles, one for each kite you need and the same again in cream cotton fabric for the linings. Place each coloured rectangle, right side up on the wadding cut to the same size and secure in place using a large running stitch all the way around the perimeter of the cotton. This will stop the two pieces sliding when machine sewing. For each kite use two contrasting gingham and bright cotton pieces to make up the kite's sections. Fold under one edge of each piece 1cm (³/₈in) and press. Now lay these pieces over the cotton and wadding rectangle. One of the pressed edges should run directly down, from top to bottom of the cotton and wadding, to form a central axis. The other should be at right angles to this. Pin to secure.

3 Set a sewing machine on a medium stitch length and topstitch over the pressed-under edges that form the central cross. Try to sew as close to these edges as possible. This will quilt (sandwich) the fabrics together. Finish all the rectangles in the same manner.

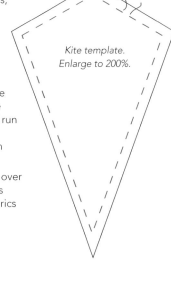

Kite template. Enlarge to 200%.

4 Right sides together, place the pre-cut lining pieces over the quilted work. Pin down matching all four of the corners. Using the template and a fabric marker, draw around the kite in the centre of each rectangle. Remove the template and place extra pins inside the kite. Do not cut anything off at the stage.

5 Using the side of the sewing machine foot as a guide, sew round the whole of the inside of the kite within the marked lines. Cut round the stitch lines leaving 5mm (¼in) seam allowance. Clip the tips of the kite. With the lining side facing you, slash a straight line about 6cm (2¼in) long in the centre from top to bottom, using fabric scissors. You now have an opening in which to turn the work through. Use a large upholstery needle or knitting needle to ease the shape of the kite to its full potential. Do not press the kites with an iron as this will flatten them. To cover up the slashed opening, draw the fabric together with a large rough stitch. Cover the drawn hole using the grosgrain ribbon. Cut the ribbon approximately 40cm (15¾in) long as this will form the kite tail. Slip stitch the ribbon into place (see page 7), covering the opening. Make sure you turn under the ribbon's raw edge just above the top of the opening for neatness. At the base of each kite tie a small bow in matching ribbon and secure into position with a hand stitch.

6 With all of the kites finished, carefully press the blue bias binding in half lengthwise, matching edge to edge. Using blue thread and a medium straight stitch machine sew the bias closed, as close to the edge as you can. Press flat. Pin the kites to the bias at the desired spacing and angle and slip stitch to the bias tape.
Clip the kite tails to the desired lengths.

Folded Flag Bunting

Materials:

Card for template

Stripy cotton, two 12 x 14cm (4¾ x 5½in) pieces per flag

2 horn buttons per flag

Red embroidery thread

White sewing thread

Cotton rope/size 6 piping to desired length of bunting plus ties

Tools:

Pencil

Ruler

Fabric marker

Pins

Scissors, both paper and fabric

Sewing machine

Large upholstery needle or knitting needle

Hand sewing needle

Flag template.
Enlarge to 200%.

Instructions:

1 Transfer the flag template on to card and cut it out. Lay your chosen stripy fabric in two layers, right sides facing. Make sure the stripes are all running in the same direction. Draw round the template with a fabric marker to make the required length of flags and cut out through both layers.

2 With the cut-outs pinned and secure, set a sewing machine to a medium-sized straight stitch and start to sew along the top of the flag. Follow the indicated stitch lines, leaving a gap to enable the work to be turned through. Carefully clip the tips and turn through, right side out. Gently tease the corners out with a large upholstery needle or knitting needle. Press flat. Repeat the process until all of the flags have been machine stitched.

3 Close the opening using a slip stitch to secure (see page 7).

4 Fold each finished piece over the top of the rope and line up the edges until you have perfect triangular flags. Use pins to hold the shape of the flag. With red embroidery thread, sew two buttons on to each flag along the top fold below the rope (otherwise the flags won't be movable). Sew through all layers so the flag is secured to the rope and remove the pins. Repeat until all of your flags are sewn over the rope.

5 It can be a good idea to have a longer rope length than intended as the flags have not been permanently attached. This allows you to space the flags closer or further apart depending on the space to be decorated.

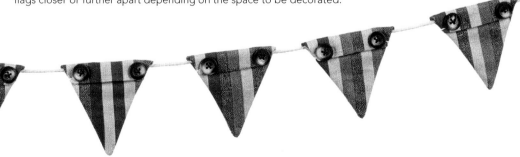

Alphabet Bunting

Materials:

Card for templates

An assortment of brightly coloured cotton fabrics, two 10 x 12cm (4 x 4¾in) pieces per flag

Brightly coloured felt scraps

Assorted coloured embroidery threads

Purple sewing thread

Bright purple bias binding 3m (3yd 10in) long and 2cm (½in) wide

Fabric glue

Tools:

Pencil

Ruler

Fabric marker

Pins

Scissors, both paper and fabric

Iron

Sewing machine

Computer and printer

Large upholstery needle or knitting needle

Hand sewing needle

Instructions:

1 Follow steps 1–3 of Floral bunting (page 8) to make the base flags. You will need twenty-six flags in total – one for each letter of the alphabet.

2 Print the whole alphabet from a computer using a clear bold font – choose to do upper or lower case. I have used a font size of 85. Use this print-out as templates for your letters. Cut out each letter in a bright coloured felt and put to one side.

3 Use a coloured embroidery thread which contrasts with the colour of each flag and hand stitch a running stitch spaced 5mm (¼in) apart and running 5mm (¼in) away from the edge. This will add decorative colour to each flag.

4 Glue a felt letter on to each flag just above the pointed tip. Allow to dry completely following the glue manufacturer's instructions.

5 Take the purple bias binding and, using an iron, carefully press in half lengthwise, matching the edges together. Sandwich each flag between the folded bias and pin into position, spacing evenly as you go; I have spaced mine 2.5cm (1in) apart. Make sure you leave enough bias at the start and finish to allow for ties. Using purple thread, machine sew the entire bunting together with a medium straight stitch. Stitch as close to the edge as you can. Easy as ABC!

Easter Bunting

Materials:

Card for templates

An assortment of brightly coloured cotton fabrics, two 8 x 11cm (3¼ x 4¼in) pieces per flag

Yellow felt

Assorted coloured embroidery threads

Assorted coloured ric-rac

Yellow sewing threads

Striped ribbon 1.5cm (½in) wide to the desired length, including ties at the ends – cut double this amount as you will be stitching this together

Fabric glue

Tools:

Pencil

Ruler

Fabric marker

Pins

Scissors, both paper and fabric

Iron

Sewing machine

Large upholstery needle or knitting needle

Hand sewing needle

Instructions:

1 Transfer the rectangle template on to card (see page 7) and cut it out. Repeat with the egg template.

2 Place each colour fabric in two layers, right sides together. Pin the rectangular template on to the fabric and draw around all of the edges with a fabric marker. Remove the template and secure the layers with pins. Cut round the marked lines. Repeat this process for all flags required.

3 Set a sewing machine to a medium-sized straight stitch. Take a flag and start to sew down one of the sides with a seam allowance 1cm (³/₈in). As you reach the end of the first side, stop the stitching 1cm (³/₈in) away from the base of the work. Lift the foot and turn the flag towards you (anti-clockwise). This will align the next side to continue stitching. Now clip the excess fabric from the tips of the flag (see page 7) and turn right side out. Use the end of a large upholstery needle or knitting needle to ease the tips of the flag out. Press flat. Repeat this process until all of the flags have been completed.

*Egg template,
actual size.*

4 With the outer edges matched, sew along the top edge of the lengths of ribbon, leaving the bottom edge open to slip in the raw edges of your flags. Leave enough ribbon at both ends to form ties. Sandwich each flag between the ribbon and secure with pins. Each flag should be 1.5cm (½in) apart.

5 Once you are happy with the arrangement and spacing, machine sew the bottom edge of the ribbon together with yellow thread, closing and trapping the flags inside. Try and sew as close to the edge as you can.

6 To make and decorate the eggs, cut out as many as you have flags in yellow felt using your egg template. Add one or two strips of ric-rac to the surface of your eggs. Attach with a running stitch and finish the ends by tucking them towards the back. Choose a brightly coloured embroidery thread and decorate the outer edge of the egg with a blanket stitch (page 6).
Glue the eggs to the flags. Allow to dry completely
before you hang the bunting.

Red, White & Blue Bunting

Materials:

Card for templates

Red, white and blue cotton fabric,
two 10 x 12cm (4 x 4¾in) pieces per triangle
and two 8 x 11cm (3¼ x 4¼in) per rectangle

Iron-on silver stars

Red sewing thread

Red bias binding 2cm (¾in) wide, measure to
the required length of the bunting, plus ties
at the ends

Tools:

Pencil

Ruler

Fabric marker

Pins

Scissors, both paper and fabric

Iron

Sewing machine

Large upholstery needle or knitting needle

Hand sewing needle

Instructions:

1 Transfer the traingle and rectangle templates (page 7) on
to card and cut them out. Each repeat of flags will make
approximately 61cm (24in) of bunting in length.

2 Lay the fabrics in double layers of eash colour; right sides
together. Pin to secure. Draw round the templates using a
fabric marker. Remove the template and secure the layers
with pins. Cut round the marked lines and, using the pattern
in the photograph as a guide, select how many of each
colour you will need and repeat this process for all the
flags required.

3 Set a sewing machine to a medium-sized straight stitch.
Take a flag and start to sew down one of the sides, with a
seam allowance of 1cm (³⁄₈in) all the way round. After sewing,
clip the excess fabric from the tips of the flag (see page 7).
Turn through the flag so it is right side out. Use the end of a
large upholstery needle or knitting needle to ease the tips of
the flag out. Press it flat and trim away the protruding seam
allowance to maintain a straight edge along the top of the
flag. Repeat for all of the flags.

4 With a hot iron, press the entire length of the bias binding in half lengthwise, taking care to match the edges for a neat finish. Leave enough bias binding at both ends to form the ties and then place the flags into position. Sandwich each flag between the binding and secure with pins. Each flag should be 2.5cm (1in) apart. Where the flags overlap, hand sew the pieces together before placing them into the binding.

5 Once you are happy with the arrangement and spacing, machine sew the bias binding together with red thread, closing and trapping the flags inside. Try and sew as close to the edge as you can. Iron on the silver stars where required.

Acknowledgements
Alistair would like to thank the team at Search Press,
including Sophie Kersey and Daniel Conway for their
editorial support, Paul Bricknell and Juan Hayward for
the beautiful photographs and staging, and to everyone
supporting me by buying a copy of my first book
– I hope you have enjoyed it!

Publisher's Note
You are invited to visit the author's website
www.houseofalistair.com.